SELLING ON AMAZON:

How to Sell on Amazon for Beginners 2020 HACKS

Learn to operate Seller Central FBA in 1 hour per day or less

Adam Wilkens

There are two kinds of companies, those that work to try to charge more and those that work to charge less. We will be the second.

JEFF BEZOS

DEDICATION

I dedicate this book to my family, my best friends,
to the loved ones I have lost but always remember,
and to my sweet dogs, Casey and Jewels.

CONTENTS

INTRODUCTION

In late 2019 I wrote a book titled "Become a Bestseller on Amazon.com" which quickly became one of the go-to 'how to sell on Amazon' books for 1st and 3rd party sellers. As a result of writing that book, I was introduced to a number of amazing new clients. I was so pleased that the response from my readers was overwhelmingly positive, thank you so much for the great reviews! The feedback from that book coupled with the dynamic (complex) nature of the Amazon platform has inspired me to write another book which will hone in on just the shortcuts needed to operate your business successfully on Amazon. com. I present to you, the 2020 SELLING ON FBA HACKERS GUIDE!

By this point I assume you have gone through sourcing and product development. You may even be an established company that feels late to the game, but now you are ready to start selling on Amazon.com.

In this short book you will learn the necessary tools so that you can operate an entire store front in as little of 1 hour per day once you have integrated your catalog into Seller Central. That is less time than you might spend getting ready for work in the morning.

With these basic skills and go-to recommendations you will dramatically improve efficiency and effectiveness. Seller Central can be the ultimate sales channel for your products or the means to providing low-maintenance passive style income.

WHAT IS SELLER CENTRAL?

Seller Central is an ecommerce platform owned by Amazon.com that allows independent sellers and merchants to list their products as available for sale on the website alongside other products that Amazon owns directly. For most shoppers they are unaware that the website is actually built up by over 50% independent sellers ranging from private citizens to actual businesses with a retail location. Think eBay, minus the bidding.

Anyone can register for Seller Central, in fact you don't even need to be a US citizen. After going through several identity confirmation steps anyone over 18 with a valid bank account, email address, official ID, and a utility bill to authenticate geolocation can register for access to their own store.

Seller Central users range from brand owners, distributors, factories overseas, and regular folks who can sell products they bought in-store for retail arbitrage or lightly used products they want to convert back to cash. It's truly a hodgepodge of agendas.

Once you, as the merchant, are a registered user you have the ability to ship products directly from your location to the customer, known as Fulfilled By Merchant (FBM). You also have the ability to ship your product(s) into the Amazon fulfillment network and make your item(s) available for Prime shipping, known as Fulfilled By Amazon (FBA).

FBA and FBM are the two methods in which you can sell and deliver products to your potential customers, and there are pros and cons to each. With FBM you control your ship speeds, you set your own pricing, and the Amazon fees on every order are more understandable as they are only based on price since they take a small commission on each sale. The downside is that your products are not available for Prime shipping, which can be a deterrent for many potential shoppers. Amazon does have a self-fulfilled Prime shipping program through FBM but they have not been accepting new applications for some time now. With FBA, Amazon controls the pick, pack, and ship and the product is listed as available with Prime shipping online, however there are more fees which can vary based on size, weight, and price. The nice part is you send them your inventory, and pretty much sit back and enjoy light order maintenance.

Regardless of which route you take Amazon does take referral fees, which can vary depending on the program. Amazon will field much of the customer service for you, however you will be expected to respond to customer questions and messages within 24 hours regardless of fulfilment method you select.

If you Google "How to Start Selling on Amazon" you can learn more about the store and its features before you sign up.

WHY USE SELLER CENTRAL?

There are many great reasons to start selling on Seller Central, but to name a few: It's cheap, easy, can make you a lot of money, it's fun, and everyone loves shopping on Amazon. You know how some gamers get paid to stream live play all day long? I get paid to play around in Seller Central all day long, and I've been doing it for over a decade. Most of the time while still in my pajamas; it is the ultimate day trader job.

For me, this is a video game. I logon, I solve puzzles, I answer questions, I look at clues to help me make my next move, and then I get paid. The difference between doing it on a part time / beginner basis (which may be some of you) vs a professional level, is that I can have two dozen saved games running at the same time. This obviously is an acquired skill-set and you need to know the system in depth so that you use every minute as efficiently possible in order to maximize your time.

Several years ago, Seller Central was still a very basic intranet which allowed re-sellers access to only the basic selling tools needed to list their products for sale on Amazon. However, over the last five years or so it has blossomed into a tool which has many, if not all of the same tools once only reserved for the largest names on the platform. From Seller Central you can manage your brand (if you own one), create a store front, run advertising campaigns, develop enhanced content for brand owners, slot promotions and coupons, upload videos, and you have access to a forecast. The Seller Central platform allows you to have access to all of these tools for the low cost of $39.99 per month. The cost is the easy part to swallow, learning how to use the platform to your benefit is the hard part. That is where I hope to show you that not only is this process easy, but with some of my hacks, I hope to help you cut down your management time into potentially an hour per day or less (varies depending on catalog size).

Now you may be asking yourself, how can Amazon make me a lot of money? The answer holds no guarantees, but a unique or popular product on the hottest marketplace on Earth will provide you with the rewards you seek. Once a product becomes popular, all of the site widgets will compound the exposure for your product. The site is all based on momentum, so assuming you can increase and hold onto that momentum you can quickly become a best-seller. As your sale rank improves so does the sales volume, and it is not uncommon for products listed in the top 100 category-wide to be selling tens of thousands of units per month. This is how you can go from an idea to quitting your day job.

One thing a lot of brand owners and re-sellers get overwhelmed with is the amount of information inside of Seller Central. When you log-in there are ten menus, settings, help sections, snap shots of metrics, alerts, and a million other bells and whistles. Most newcomers login and turn into a deer in headlights, but in the next few chapters I will go over the quick version of navigating your Amazon business so that you can cut through the complications and manage the business with speed and efficiency.

BRAND REGISTRY & BRAND MANAGEMENT

I n this chapter we will outline simple brand building on Amazon.com. If you do not have your own brand and you are strictly a distributor or reseller on Seller Central then you may skip ahead of this chapter. If you have a brand or are in the process of registering your trademark, then you will want to know some of these brand hacks in order to: save time, create less work, and have less headaches.

There are two types of trademarks issued by the United States Patent Office (USPTO), the word mark and the design mark. The word mark is registered to the combination of letters and numbers, generally agnostic of capitalization, for specific categories of products or services offered. The design mark is a registration of a logo typically, or a unique design as it relates to a given brand. Amazon Brand Services allows for registration of either mark as proof of brand ownership on their platform. By linking the registration or trademark owner back from USPTO they can verify that you do indeed own your brand. If you have either or both marks you can register them at brandservices.Amazon.com.

Registration is easy once you navigate to the site, there will be several enrollment links and a form to initially fill out which confirms your legal name, business address, business name, and 2SV (two step verification)

HACK # 1 - Make sure when you click to Enroll Your Brand you are logged into Amazon.com using the exact same email address as you have registered as the primary store owner on Seller Central.

HACK # 2 - When you are completing the form to enroll your brands make sure that the exact spelling, spacing, capitalization, matches 100% to what is shown on the detail page in the title. There is a blue hyperlink under your title, whatever that capitalization/spacing/spelling is must match what you provide in your application.

HACK # 3 - When you get the congratulations email from Brand Registry confirming your brand has been registered, wait 24-48 hours and then log back in to brand registry, and create a "technical issue" case asking them to sync your brand to your merchant token associated with your seller store. You can find this Merchant Token by going to Seller Central, "Settings" → "Account Info" → "Business Information" → "Merchant Token."

If you have done all of these things correctly then you have accomplished several major obstacles that brand owners struggle with, which is registration of your brand, avoiding future corrections to the brand name, and the brand sync'ing to their store. What you have now accomplished is claiming ownership of the brand and told Amazon, "Hey, my store has control over this brand, and not a random reseller."

It is a wise move to create the brand registry before creating any products because otherwise you have to complete another fun project, which is syncing your brand to your ASIN list. The only way to do this is to do what Amazon refers to as a "full catalog update." If you want to understand how to do this, create a new technical issue ticket in Seller Central and ask for instructions on this. It will require you to use the inventory upload tool from the "Inventory" → "Add products via Upload" menu.

The item update file will be the best way for you to stay organized with your assortment. Think of it as your master item information file. It will include the important details for every aspect of your product detail page. Keep this file in a safe place on your computer because any time you need to make product description changes this handy file will be your go to. It can be a little bit of a bear understanding what each field means, along with how to use it. If you are at all concerned what to do with it, how to start, where to use it then stop everything you are doing and create a support ticket using the 'Get Support' link at the bottom left of every page or the top right of every page under 'Help.'

HACK # 4 - Always create a ticket if you are lost. The vendor support is free, so use it as much as possible. It's easier and more efficient to ask for help then struggle and get frustrated with your experience selling on Amazon.

At this point you have accomplished a lot with your trademark on Amazon! We assume you have created ASINs or refreshed the brand sync on your existing ASINs, have access to your brand(s) in the Brand Registry portal. If the store sync was successful, you should now have the ability to create a 'Store' under this menu in Seller Central by clicking 'Manage Store,' but if you can not then you will need to create a ticket and ask for access to all of the brand tools on your seller store, they should be able to fix any issues for you.

The creation of your store is important because it is the face of your company to Amazon shoppers. Many brand owners forget to do this, or they push the project off for months or years. Your store is important; it tells customers who you are, what you sell, and they will be looking for it. Blockbuster video would not have dominated the video rental market in the 80's if they had no sign hanging up outside the building. The store page on Amazon is the equivalent of your sign on the outside of a retail building, it says come inside and browse.

The best part about the store is that it is simple to use and the entire setup is template-based. If you have access to simple photo editing software you can make any banners you need to fill in the blanks. If you don't have any editing software, the template will display the exact size dimensions you need for each module so that you can outsource it to a graphic designer. After a few revisions and drafts, you can publish and have the store live within 24 hours.

Another nice feature of the store is that you can even pick your store, URL. Once you have an approved store make sure that the little blue link that has your brand name, located under the product title, links back to the published brand store. It should. They call this little blue link the brand byline. If it's not linking to your store, make a case and ask them to fix it.

Once some of this groundwork is done, you may never have to play around with it again. Of course, anytime you add new products or do any major design updates you will want to make changes, but for many of you this brand page is essentially a set it and forget it situation.

When it comes to brand management itself there are many small components of creating a cohesive brand, that many sellers neglect.

HACK # 5 - You should be habitually checking the brand byline for functionality. Regularly click on this link to make sure it is not broken or is not a hyperlink to another unrelated brand.

You should also be taking advantage of a comparative chart as the last module of A+ content / EMC (enhanced merchandising content) on every ASIN in your assortment. This way you can more easily provide customers the ability to cross-shop your own catalog without ever hitting the back button and leaving your detail page, once they leave the odds are high, they do not return. We will discuss A+ / EMC in depth in later chapters.

Make sure your images, alternate images, banners, and marketing materials show cohesion between the brand and all of its proucts. The familiarity will help develop your brand as an Amazon "household brand." Car makers have been doing this for years, you always know when you are looking at a Volvo or a Volkswagen, they all have the same look. The Fords and the Chevy's all have the same grill styling, etc.

Your brand style needs to look familiar and all part of the same family. When you create a hodgepodge of brand aesthetics it disturbs the ability for customers to connect the dots. Recall and familiarity amongst your brand style will not be as easy, this becomes especially important if the product is something that lends itself to regular re-ordering through none-subscription-based re-ordering of products.

Find a graphic artist with a flare you like, and use them for all of your photography and graphic design, this way you guarantee consistency.

HACK # 6 - Look at your existing catalog and then double it by offering variations of item-count, size, or color.

Conduct regular reviews of your product assortment and ordering behavior to determine what items can be bundled to offer more quantity, value, or options for the customer. If you see certain items are being bought in two's and three's then you should be creating a pre-bundled two or three pack ASINs as a new child variation. The same goes for larger sizes of product that are liquid for example, increasing the ounce size is a good option for a secondary item. If you are selling a product with color variations, consider expanding the color options to give customers a larger selection to choose from. People like options!

Keep in mind every time you add new items you will want to update your brand page and potentially your A+ content comparative chart module. This way you can help funnel more traffic from your best sellers to your slow sellers and also cross-sell amongst your own brand rather than a competing brand.

Cohesion amongst your brand needs to be locked down so that you catch customers in a big loop. They just keep browsing between your assortment until they buy within your assortment. The brand page byline needs to work so they can visit your store, see your products, click on products. The tables and variants always bring them back to more of your products. The widgets for "frequently bought with" also show more of your items combined. You want it to be like groundhog's day with a big loop until they convert with the least amount of thinking or fewest clicks to the sale as possible. Easy and clear messaging helps expedite the purchase. When you get too confusing people flee.

We will discuss advertising in a later chapter but for the purpose of understanding the basic principles on how pay per click (PPC) impacts your branding, I will briefly elaborate here before touching on it again later.

Part of your advertising spend needs to be dedicated to sponsored brand ads which help promote the overall brand through banners placed under the search bar. You should be using a combination of the sponsored brand ads to drive people to the store with an overall brand campaign, another sponsored brand ad that is product-type specific, along with a series of sponsored product ads which pepper themselves into the search results. This will help you develop organic relevance through artificially influencing search results and in doing so will make your brand more prevalent to category-specific and brand-specific keyword searches.

The artificial relevance (paid keyword advertising) all feels like organic relevance to the Amazon algorithm over time, so by manipulating the system and converting sales on keywords the algorithm sees you as relevant on those terms once you develop increased sales momentum on those terms.

HACK # 7 - Bid high on your brand terminology to prevent anyone else from appearing but you. Own your own terms!

NEW ITEM LAUNCH LIST

I f you have ever been on one of my webinar interviews you have heard me discuss the *holy grail new item launch list*. This is a formula which I have been using for the better part of the last decade to successfully launch ASINs for my customers, which have generated millions of dollars in revenue. The secret sauce can now be yours for free; well for the cost of purchasing this book.

The first step will be to write out your title, 5 description rich bullet features, and paragraph style product descriptions. You can begin working on this project once you are in the product development phase or in production. Keep them as lengthy as possible but also stay within the category character count allowance for your browse-node (sub-category).

HACK # 8 - If you want to use an "Amazon HTML style product description" you can Google that phrase and find several free tools where you can plug in your text and it will automatically code the product description to HTML for use on Amazon.

1) Item title, bullets, and product description:

   • Title 200-250 characters.

   • 5 bullet features up to 250 characters in length.

- Product description 2000 characters total.

- To be completed 2-3 weeks before inventory availability.

The second step after you have post production samples is to arrange a photoshoot. Once you have raw images you can have your photographer add rich infographics to the alternate images to include some of the selling materials found in your bullet features. The only reason you want a little bit of redundancy here is because some customers would rather read along with the images like a story book, it's easier than weeding through long bullet features.

Video is optional and is a good supplement to your main and alternate images. Keep the video brief but helpful. Do not include any outside linking to your website and avoid any guarantees, promises, sales, promotional language, adult material, or competitor names and you should be ok.

2) Images and video:

- 1 Main Image Solid White Background.

- 6-7 alternate images with infographics.

- 1 video 30-45 seconds at most.

- To be completed 2-3 weeks before inventory availability.

The third step is adding the product to Seller Central and you can do that one of two ways. The easiest being under "Inventory" → "Add a Product." From here the system will require you to first search for the ASIN to guarantee it does not already exist on the website, this is to reduce the likelihood of duplicate ASIN creation. Once the system has determined the item does not exist, you can go through the process of using the template-based item builder to fill out all of the necessary item data until you are ready to submit. The second way to create new items is slightly more complicated, and requires you to download an item setup file through "Inventory" → "Add Products Via Upload." Through this method you are downloading a file specific to the category-type of the ASIN(s) you are creating. All of your item data goes on this file and then you upload it to create your item. It can be more problematic and error-prone however it makes updates significantly easier in the future and also guarantees you complete the ASIN sync to your brand as mentioned earlier in the Brand Registry chapter.

3) Add item to Seller Central

- Create 3rd party offer for FBM and FBA.

- Send small amount of inventory to FBA (optional).

- To be completed once inventory is available.

The fourth step is A+ content (EMC) and is a very important part of the puzzle. If we compare your detail page to that of a small product brochure then the main and alternate images would be the cover and the A+ content description will be the interior of that brochure. The purpose is to keep potential shoppers interested in the product(s) so that they stay on your detail page and eventually buy (convert). The A+ content provides supplemental sales material to really sell the product(s) and reduce the risk of the customer leaving the detail page. Do not use redundant sales language here or the same images used in your main and alternates, this is meant to be additional sales material not repetitive sales material.

4) A+ content:

- Brand Banner for module #1.

- Supporting tile images (differ from main and alternates).

- Supporting description for each tile image.

- Use all 7 modules for A+ content.

- To be completed 2-3 weeks before inventory availability.

The fifth step is the Early Reviewer Program (ERP) is a program that costs $60 and allows for room of up to 5 reviews on a product that otherwise has none. When you agree to fund the program cost of $60, Amazon will send emails to customers post-purchase enticing them with an offer to receive a few dollars if they agree to leave a product review. This is a good way to generate your first few reviews for a very low cost, and since the first reviews are the hardest to get this program is a no brainer. More details can be located under

5) ERP Early reviewer program:
- Enroll Item in Early Reviewer Program for $60 cost.
- To be completed once inventory is available.

The sixth step is your Advertising. I will outline this subject later in the book, however understanding the framing of advertising and how it relates to item launch is important now. When new items are created, they have no search or sales history, this also means they have no relevance. When an item has no relevance, it does not appear on page one of search results for most of the category-related search terms necessary to drive sales. In order to artificially stimulate impressions on page one for those important category terms, we need to pay for those clicks. Over time paying for enough clicks that translate into sales, help with your keyword relevance. If you build it, they may not come. This is why we need to turn on those ads now to get glance views to your detail page(s) and get sales. If you wait for organic traffic that could take a long time. This is like a B12 shot to the arm.

6) PPC Advertising:

- Create Sponsored Product Ads (SPA) - manual and automatic targeting.

- Create headline search ads.

- Create product ads.

- Launch with video ads.

- To be completed once inventory is available.

The seventh step is related to Promotions and Deals. Seller Central allows for several types of Promotions, Deals, and Coupons. You can find these opportunities and recommendations under the Advertising menu. From "Advertising" → "Promotions" you can schedule a promo-code, free-shipping, percentage off, or BOGO (buy one get one) promotions. Run experimentations on what works for you, be careful not to overlap promotions so that you are not creating a situation where multiple discounts are running at once. Deals are good calls to action, once the customer gets to the detail page via your ad, they will see your great content, be interested in the product, and then enticed to buy with a limited time discount. These things will create urgency and reduce the amount of thinking necessary to convert to a sale.

I always suggest running some sort of discount first and then intermittently follow up with a coupon or another deal. You will want some periods in-between where the item is at regular price. The goal is to increase your momentum during a sale so that the rank and sell-through is elevated afterwards when the product is being sold at its regular MSRP. They call this a halo-effect.

Once your product begins to sell well, Amazon will make recommendations for performing ASINs to be invited to participate in Lightning Deals. You will see these recommendations under the "Advertising" → "Deals" menu. Items without high sales-volume potential, an underperforming star-rating, or with inventory shortage issues do not qualify.

7) Promotions & Deals
   - Schedule a discount promotion.
   - Schedule coupon 2-4 weeks after the deal ends.
   - To be completed once inventory is available.

HACK # 9 - It's all about traffic! The more traffic you generate through ads / images / words / promotions then the

higher your odds are to convert traffic into sales. Traffic =
Sales

You need glance views, so everything you can do to increase traffic will likely increase sales. If you can assist traffic from outside sources such as social media or your website then do that as well. All of these things combine to increase your relevance. Once you start to increase this sales momentum you are then picked up by all of the little sales widgets on site, which again compound sales. This includes flags for Amazon's choice, best seller, movers and shakers, visibility on the deals page, visibility on the category landing page, wish lists, and more. All of these little metric based widgets help you sell more product.

PPC ADVERTISING

A few short years ago, Amazon.com decided to offer a CPC (cost per click) advertising model to help sellers create artificial relevance for an ASIN, and it has since exploded into one of the fastest growing ad platforms on the internet. The purpose is to provide an additional way to drive traffic and promote awareness about your detail pages. The program first began as an exclusive to 1P vendors only (Vendor Central) but has since become widely used by 3P vendors on the Seller Central platform as well. Within the Amazon advertisement family, you have control over all advertising and your Brand Store (formally Brand Page) for your brand(s) sold on Amazon.com.

Historically, there are three primary ad types, and each has unique placements on Amazon.com:

- Sponsored Product Ads (SPA): Appear in search results and detail pages.

- Sponsored Brand Ads (Formally HSA): Appear as a banner immediately below search results.

- Product Display Ads (PDA): Appear only on your products' or competitors' detail page

HACK # 10 - In the last six months to a year, a new Sponsored Video Ad has now become available whereby you can upload a 15 second clip which appears as a dynamic au-to-playing video inside search results. I would encourage you to use this since it is new. Early adopters are always rewarded.

Amazon advertising is definitely a science, and I will be the first to tell you that it is the most complex part of marketing a product for sale on Amazon.com. It is 100% necessary at this stage in the game because it is so heavily used by the largest players in every category. If you do not compete in this space on keywords relevance, you could potentially lose relevance to a newcomer who does everything you are currently doing plus has the skills and/or budget to outpace you on the advertising front.

Rather than go into how to create ads, and what each ad does, I am going to make the recommendation to read through the help section on AMS. This will give you a good understanding of what each ad does, where it shows up, and how to create an ad which is super simple. There are also some great videos on YouTube; AMS has their own channel, and there are several videos out there for creating ads with AMS. I highly encourage you to watch the 3-5 videos created by AMS on the three ad types. Creating ads is the easiest part as it's basically adding keywords to existing preset (template-based) content, bid pricing, and budget pricing.

Strategy is the part you cannot read about, and it's also the part that you will not learn from your competition because AMS data is private to the manufacturer. This is a principle I have learned over the course of having multiple close relationships with AMS team members since the inception of the advertising platform.

Before we can go in-depth on strategy, we need to understand the fundamental reasons why AMS works as a supplement to organic search elements (detail page content). The two most influential ad types (Sponsored product ads and Sponsored brand ads) appear within the Search Engine Page Results (SERP) when a customer uses the product search tool. As the customer shops and the SERP display results for products with the most organic relevance, the ads (artificial results) are peppered in with organic items tied to the original keywords used to search. Basically, you are force-feeding a page one or two impression on a customer that you may not otherwise have. This is important because 70% of all sales occur from page 1 results. The other 30% of sales are page two. Beyond page three and you are in the no-man zone, sales drop off a cliff from there.

There is a flowchart of processes that starts when a customer enters search terms and ends when that customer makes a purchasing choice to "buy-it now." The funnel flow exists whether or not the customer is exposed to an ad, or not exposed to an ad. If we do not have any page one exposure on a given search term, then the ad influence over the funnel becomes the most important piece in this puzzle. Maybe your ASIN lacks enough organic relevance to be on page one, but why wait for that to happen? You can pay for impressions on page one and kickstart the funnel process to grab some of those lost opportunities and build rank.

The impacts of Amazon advertising on the funnel; how and when the customers are exposed to the product or brands in combination with any organic product relevance will help compound sales for any manufacturer who uses these tools.

The Amazon.com Brand Store tool works very similar to the A+ content tool. There are a number of prearranged pages, you can add pages, you can add page sections, or you can opt to customize the whole thing. If you have a marketing manager or an in-house graphic artist, I would assign them permissions to Seller Central (Advertising & Brand Store management) so that they can login and access the tool to create the Brand Store.

If you have any issues at all, create a support ticket. For fastest access to answers select the phone option rather than email. The agent will be able to assist you with adding another user and also be able to answer any troubleshooting issues you have with Brand Store creation. In Seller Central you will need to go to the menu for "Advertising & Stores" → "Stores" → "Basic Settings"

Note that in order to create the brand store you will have to complete Brand Registry

Once you have your Brand Store created, you are now ready to begin advertising it. At this point, you need to determine what product(s) you want to advertise and what your total budget is. Knowing your total budget will help determine how you spread it around. Most ad budgets are set based on a daily spend; the daily budget may not always be maximized each day but so that you-do not get any surprises on your next credit card statement, just assume it could spend the max daily budget. For example, if you set your ad budget for $25.00 per day, expect that it may spend that each day. Especially if the campaign is on Automatic settings.

My suggestion is to determine a monthly budget that works for you. If it is $1000 per month, then you know you have a total of $33 per day to play with. The smaller the budget you have, the harder it becomes to have good coverage with Amazon advertising as you likely need to divide your total daily budget into several ad types or product types.

HACK # 11 - Amazon says that an ad with a $50 daily budget or more is the least likely to run out of the budget.

It is recommended that 40-50% of your budget is on sponsored product ads, 40-50% of your budget is on sponsored brand ads, and 10-20% of your budget is on product display ads. You may be going, hey that is more than 100%. Keep in mind it is not an exact science; you may find that you are more weighted in sponsored product ads vs. sponsored brand ads, it all depends on what works best for you based on your ACOS (advertising cost of sale) and sales. I personally like 45% SPA, 45% SBA, and 10% PDA.

The product display ads will always be the least performing and least cost-effective ad type. Therefore, you only want it to be a small portion of your budget.

Let's say you have a product named 'ABC widget.' Here is how you will want to create your campaigns for 'ABC widget' to maximize "the success of the ads and provide the clarity by outlining the purpose of each ad campaign."

For each product, create 4 ads per sponsored product ads

- SPA Ad #1) Competitor Terms Ad
- SPA Ad #2) Branded Terms Ad
- SPA Ad #3) Category Terms Ad
- SPA Ad #3) Automatic Targeting

For each product, create 4 sponsored brand ads:

- SBA Ad #1) Competitor Terms Ad
- SBA Ad #2) Branded Terms Ad
- SBA Ad #3) Category Terms Ad
- SBA Ad #3) Automatic Targeting

For each product, create 1-2 product display ads:

- PDA Ad #1) Product Targeting
- PDA Ad #2) Category Targeting

In your Competitor Terms ads, you will have only keywords specific to rival products and brands, for example, if you worked for Pepsi, then your competitor terms would be: Coke, Coca-Cola, Coke Zero, RC cola, etc.

In your Category Terms ads, you will only have keywords that are specific to the product type or category, no brand-specific terms, no product specific terms, and ZERO terms relating to your products' name or brand name. i.e., makeup, cosmetics, cleaning supplies, donuts, ties.

In your Branded Terms ads, you will have only keywords that are specific to your brand name(s) and your product names, along with every variation that you can think of. Include misspellings.

Your automatic ad is used to cast a wide net and fill in the blanks for any keywords you may be missing in the other three ad groupings. For example, you may download the automatic-ad report and discover that there was a sale on a Category Term you don't currently have in your ads, so you manually add it in.

HACK # 12- Keywords are ranked in order of importance by exact, phrase, and then broad type.

Setting Budgets on Keywords Types:

The rationale is that Exact Keyword Matches outweigh Phrase Match Keywords, which outweigh Broad Match Keywords. With this in mind, you will want to add all keywords into each ad type in redundancy, so each keyword will be added three times with the only variables being 'keyword type' and bid amount for each use of the same keyword.

So, the word "Pepsi" would be added as broad, phrase, and exact into the Branded Terms ads.

Start the bidding at all broad terms at $1.00, then $1.50 for phrase type, and then $2.00 for exact types

KEYWORD	MATCH TYPE	BID AMOUNT
Pepsi	Broad	$1.00
Pepsi	Phrase	$1.50
Pepsi	Exact	$2.00

The purpose of this exercise is to see which keyword type is the most efficient way for you to bid on the keyword, and the best metric of making this determination is the ACOS percentage. If one is 200% and another is 40%, then you can pause the expensive options and continue on with your lower cost keyword types (for the same keyword) in order to maximize your budget efficiency. I like ACOS over sales because ACOS is the total sales divided by total spend. So, if you spent $10 but generated $100, your ACOS should be 10%.

It is important to note that all sales have a 14-day sales attribution window. If an ad made an impression on someone on day one, the customer clicked the ad, purchased any product in your assortment, then that sale will be credited to the ad. If a sale is made on the 15th day or further from the original click, then the ad will not be able to record that sale.

Once you create your ads, you will need two weeks before your first adjustments. If you have an assigned Amazon Advertising Representative, then I would advise you speak with them regarding bulk optimizations. They can send you reports as often as every week or every other week to optimize all of your ads with a simple bulk upload file, for additional questions relating to this, please create a 'contact us' ticket or speak with your advertising rep.

Manual Adjustments to Bids and Budgets:

This is where things get complex and a little tricky, a lot of this is personal preference and budget dependent. I am going to lay out how I manage my bids and budget changes.

If you are looking to make a big splash on the impression in a short time frame, you can select auto budgeting with a very high daily or max budget and the AI will plow through that budget, delivering the most amount of impressions it can within the set time frame. This way, you can literally make millions of impressions in a day if you wanted, but it will not be efficient.

If you are going for efficiency, I would recommend you do the following as it concerns raising and lowering the bid amounts.

If ACOS is over 100% I would consider several things:

- If this keyword is directly related to the products, then reduce the bid price below $.50 CPC.

- If the keyword is a redundancy and the alternate keyword types on the same keyword are cheaper, then pause this one

- If the keyword is not related to the product directly but on a fringe or outlier, pause.

- If the keyword is the most important keyword you have and over 100% ACOS on all broad, phrase, and exact then keep the lowest ACOS version and continue to spend money on this keyword until relevance improves but know that it will likely suck up a lot of your budget. If you spend enough time and money on a keyword that ACOS will come down, but it may be very inefficient in the process. Some vendors do not care. For example, if you were Nest, and you wanted to spend whatever it took on the word "Thermostat" because that is your most valuable keyword, but its ACOS is 257% then you are going to keep throwing cash at that keyword until sales improve to a point where you are relevant to "Thermostat."

If ACOS is 40% + I would consider several things:

- Reduce bid amount on a keyword by 10-20%, do this every couple of weeks until the ACOS decreases then hold.

- Leave it alone, because your strategy is to buy relevance. It will come at a cost and reduce over time.

- Follow bid suggestions to reduce CPC and make less modifications/tracking of changes.

- Pause keyword if one of the other match types has a lower ACOS.

If ACOS is 20-30% I would consider several things:

- Increase bids by 10% - see if ACOS changes in two weeks.

- Hold.

- Pause other match types on the same keyword if they have a higher ACOS.

- Check bid suggestions vs. ACPC.

If ACOS is 10-20% I would consider several things:

- Increase bids by 10-20% and check ACOS in two weeks.

- Pause other match types on sale keyword if they have a higher ACOS.

- See if bid suggestions are higher than a 20% increase, if they are, then follow those suggestions.

If ACOS is < 10% I would consider several things:

- Double the bid and check in two weeks what has changed (If anything with ACOS).

- Pause other match types on sale keyword if they have a higher ACOS unless under 20% then leave them.

- Check bid suggestions.

HACK # 13 - Tips and Tricks for your ad strategy:

- Use a starting bid over $5.00 on anything that is your own brand name, you should naturally have the most relevance for your own brand and therefore own this term. The high bid price will guarantee ownership of the term. Increase if necessary.

- On all major holidays such as Prime Day or November-December consider increASINg bids and daily budgets by 2-4X.

- If you are receiving email notifications that you are running out of budget, then you need to increase the daily budgets in small increments to stretch the dollar so that it lasts longer in the day. As you approach holiday season with low budgets, you can expect your entire budget to run out by 8-10am PST in some cases.

- If you are bidding on keywords that have a high traffic potential but you are not generating many impressions, and generating no sales this means your bids are too low. Check the column for ACPC; this is the average CPC of that keyword. You are likely not bidding competitively.

- If you are bidding over the ACPC but generating no sales then you are not relevant, you can reduce the bid price to a level in line with the ACPC or pause the keyword so that you do not waste budget.

- Make small changes and track your changes to learn what works and what doesn't.

- Some categories have high ROAS (return on ad spend), and some have low returns. For example, in beauty, I would be happy with a lifetime ACOS of 35-45%, and this is because the ACPC for some keywords is over $4.00 CPC. Which is insane, but that's the reality.

- If an advertising specialist reaches out to you, get them to commit to meetings every two weeks to review your campaigns.

- If you choose not to advertise, someone else will. Avoiding advertising will make it more difficult for you to compete in your space when the rest of your competition is. Factor advertising into your COGS (cost of goods sold).

- If a keyword has a lower ACOS on one match type vs. the other(s), keep the one with the lowest ACOS and pause or delete the others. i.e., an exact match is 15% ACOS vs. a Broad match 25% ACOS on the same keyword; you would then pause the broad match.

- To continue incremental growth on Amazon, search advertising alone will not allow you to maintain continuous incremental growth. Talk with your Amazon advertising rep about displays ads, also known as "AMG," to get yourself "outside the aisle" and find new customers not currently in-market for your products.

- NEW as of 2019 - You will notice there is an "Apply" button next to your bids, if you click this for each keyword the system will automatically optimize you somewhere between the lowest and highest ACPC bid range if it thinks you should decrease or increase your ads. Use this with caution. It seems to be more efficient when suggesting downward bids rather than upward bids. Don't blindly click apply and accept all recommendations.

- NEW since 2019 - "BID +" feature has been replaced by 'dynamic bidding.' Within your ads "Campaign Settings" there is a feature for "Campaign bidding Strategy" this allows the system to 'bid up or down' your bid presets if it thinks it can secure a sale. These are the newest bidding options that replaced Bid+:

1. 'Dynamic Bids - down only' - only lowers your bids if it thinks you are less likely to get a sale.

2. 'Dynamic Bids - up and down' - will raise your bids over 100% pre-set bid amount if the system thinks it can get the sale, and also lower your bids when you are less likely to get a sale.

3. 'Fixed Bids' - it will not make any changes to your bidding at all, ever.

I like to stick with option #1 as I think this provides for the most efficiency based on what I have seen.

A+ CONTENT (EMC)

A+ content for marketplace vendors provides the ability for manufacturers (brand owners only) to place a digital product catalog on the detail page of an ASIN below the product description. The purpose is to provide continued interaction with the customer in an effort to prevent detail page abandonment and ultimately drive more sales to the detail page. From personal experience, I have seen effective A+ content drive sales an additional 5-15% over time depending on the product type and rank. The A+ content is used to drive product education and overall brand awareness via rich content, images, and comparative charts. Amazon has a number of templates available to suit the needs of any product and some or all of the features within each template can be used or ignored, including headers, bullet features, watermarks, images, keywords, and paragraphs.

A+ content is free for all manufacturers with a brand registry approved trademark"

HACK # 14 - Amazon allows for a maximum of 7 stacked modules, USE THEM UP! Don't only provide the bare minimum and post A+ content with 1 or 2 modules. Your competitors are lazy, they won't use them all!

Always go above and beyond. Amazon knows that A+ content drives sales and ultimately aids conversion, so this decision to open up the A+ modules at no expense to the seller (except time) is in their best interest. Whether you have a large catalog or a small catalog, I highly encourage you to make this time investment. It will require custom artwork with the use of photo editing software and some time to write the "Romance Language" or marketing copy for the A+ content itself, but the end result will be permanent and worth your efforts. The beautiful thing about A+ content is that you can edit the content within Seller Central on a self-service basis. You do not need to create a ticket.

A+ content is also a valuable search engine optimization (SEO) tool, more so for search engines than specifically on Amazon.com itself. Amazon says that the A+ content SEO impacts search engines such as Google, Yahoo, and Bing, etc. The interesting part is that I am told that the hidden keywords imbedded within the images may impact search similar to how "hidden keywords" do on the detail page. My suggestion is to max out all of the keywords imbedded within the A+ content images with language that you may not have used elsewhere on the detail page, such as competitor products, broad search language relating to the product, and some narrow search directly related to the product terms as well.

A+ content is great for products in variation and will be a valuable tool in conveying to customers the difference between product families and options. For example, if you have a Good-Better-Best product catalog, you will want to include all of these in the A+ by using a comparison chart with product specifications between the family and links to those other products. You can also use the charge to convey product differences by family or type. You can expose shoppers to totally different product types in your own assortment, there are no rules to how you can use the chart to sell other products in your catalog. Get creative!

By employing this method, you are providing customers additional options without the need for them to back out of the detail page and go on with search results. You want them to continue clicking on your own brand until they make a purchase regardless of whether they are upsold or down sold. At the end of the day, a sale is a sale, and it all helps with rank, product awareness, and product loyalty.

HACK # 15 - Do not use the same images from your main and alternates in the body of the A+ content. Upload fresh new lifestyle images which show the product in use. These additional images will help paint the picture of the potential customer owning/using the product.

VIDEO UPLOADS

Assuming you have unlocked the special tools reserved for registered brands, you should also have access to upload videos to your detail pages. You can locate this menu by navigating to "Inventory" → "Upload and Manage Videos". If you have successfully made it to this page it says "Manage Videos" in the upper left corner.

The process of adding video is very easy. If you click "Upload Video" it will walk you through steps to drag and drop your video into the center of the screen. It has a field for the video title (which must be fewer than 60 characters), another field where you can enter one or more ASIN(s) to apply the video to, and an option for a thumbnail cover image which will act like a still shot on the detail page.

Acceptable video formats are .mp4 and .mov and must be under 500MB in total size. They recommend a 480P resolution or better for quality. Amazon has quite a bit of content policies, and your video can be removed or rejected for violating any of these.

HACK # 16 - Before you film your video please do a search in the "Help" section for a subject of "Video Content Policy" so you understand what you can and cannot say or show in the video.

I cannot tell you how many times I have been supplied a video and it is later rejected because it does not meet the video guidelines.

Amazon is very conservative when it comes to product claims, promotions, comparisons with competitor products, violence, nudity, sexuality, guarantees and warranties (using the word cheap, sale, promotion), included use of reviews or ratings, asking for reviews, false or misleading language. Videos cannot be marketed towards children or intended to deceive. There is a laundry list of things you can't say or do, more things you cannot do vs can do. With all of this in mind, it is best to read the guidelines and then provide all of that to your videographer prior to filming or editing of your video.

HACK # 17 - Videos do not hold the same weight as Images or length descriptions on Amazon. My suggestion is to think about videos last, they will not have the same number of clicks or views as images or A+ content.

In some cases, as on the PC platform (not the mobile Amazon app), the video has a special hiding space below the fold and customers may rarely even see it. It is my professional opinion that the video is a nice finishing touch but it is not necessary. I would add one to every detail page, however I would focus on it last.

The nice thing about Amazon videos are that they can also be implemented on your brand page, just in a slightly different max size. On the brand page they advise your video must be at least 1,280 x 640 pixels, and less than 100MB. Avi, mov, mpg, mpeg, mp4, m4a, m4v, and m4p files are supported. You can also use a cover image for this brand page video which must be 3000x1500 pixels.

REVIEWS, CUSTOMER SERVICE, AND STORE FEEDBACK

Reviews are an interesting aspect of Amazon, and outside of price, an important metric by which customers base their purchASINg on. If you have thousands of reviews and mediocre content, you can still move tonnage because you have default credibility, even if the product is a sham. Generating reviews has to be one of your most sought-after goals while doing business with Amazon.com. In this chapter, we will discuss a few things.

1. What are the Amazon policies for customer reviews?

2. How can you combat negative reviews?

3. How can I generate more reviews on my own?

4. How can I generate more reviews with the help of an outside service?

5. What are the Amazon policies for reviews?

HACK # 18 - There are several helpful links that every seller should read as it concerns reviews. You can find both of them in the "Help" section by searching for "Review Guidelines", "Customer Reviews", and "Customer Product Reviews Policy."

Amazon does not allow self-promotions, profanity, slander, reviews in exchange for money or free products, racism, sexual content, illegal or fraudulent activity, or manipulation/abuse of the review system. Any suspicious reviews which include variations of the above non-allowed behavior can be flagged by Amazon or other customers for review or removal.

Below are a few examples of reviews types that Amazon does not allow:

- A product manufacturer posts a review of their own product, posing as an unbiased shopper
- A shopper, unhappy with their purchase, posts multiple negative reviews for the same product
- A customer posts a review in exchange for $5
- A customer posts a review of a game, in exchange for bonus in-game credits
- A family member of the product creator posts a five-star customer review to help boost sales
- A shopper posts a review of the product, after being promised a refund in exchange
- A seller posts negative reviews on his competitor's product
- An artist posts a positive review on a peer's album in exchange for receiving a positive review from them.

How can you Combat Negative Reviews?

Reviews can be disputed, which is a nice thing. You cannot just remove any 1-star review because you don't like what the customer has to say, unfortunately. It doesn't work that way. The only way you can remove reviews is if the reviewer has violated one of the Amazon policies. This can get tricky, and it is a delicate situation.

HACK # 19 - If you think Amazon removed a customer review that they shouldn't have, please e-mail review-appeals@Amazon.com . If you feel there is a review on your product(s) that Amazon should consider removing, you may appeal it by contacting Amazon.com at community-help@Amazon.com . Additionally, you can also create a ticket in Seller Central; there are sub-topics options which you can select to contact them about reviews.

If you think reviews are suspicious and seem like spam, then make a clear case to the review team why the review should be removed. For example, if you feel the product was potentially damaged in shipping, or maybe the customer bought a used product from a 3rd party seller whose identity you can't confirm nor the origin of the product.

Always make sure to include a copy of the permalink for the review, the reviewer's name, and the ASIN the review relates to. If you hear back from Community Reviews that the review does not violate any of the Amazon terms, then you should reach out to the customer and initiate a dialogue using the official manufacturer review tool/process.

Make sure you are logged into Seller Central as an admin with your business account. Do not be logged into Amazon under your personal account. From here you can click on the review in question on the Amazon.com homepage. Below the review, you will see a link that says "Comment." This is how you will enter into a dialogue with the customers. The key is to kill them with kindness so that other potential shoppers see that you offer good customer service, are making an attempt to resolve the issue, and potentially offer solutions that negate the poor review.

I always tell my clients to structure several canned responses depending on the product problem. For example, if it was an install or assembly error, you can say something along the lines of "Hello, I am really sorry to hear that you are having a problem assembling ABC widget. In the user manual, on page 4, we offer instructions on how to connect those two parts. If you are still having problems we would love to talk with you to make sure that you can enjoy ABC widget, please reach us by phone at 800123-4567 or via email at customerservice@inserthere.com" or you can ask the customer to contact you offline for a free replacement right in the review if the product is inexpensive and has a known issue. Essentially anything you can do to ease the fears for new shoppers or clear up any basic misunderstandings with product features without being accusatory. The key to success here is to remember that you are leaving a permanent and very public response to this customer review, so you want to avoid any arguments, defensiveness, or attitude.

After you leave the comment, it may appear with a notation next to the comment as "manufacturer." If it does not say this, or show your company name (vendor name), then you may want to create a case for this and refer to it as the "official manufacturer comment feature." They have renamed this feature several times as well as how the feature works, best to ask in a ticket so you further understand how and when it can be used.

HACK # 20 - How can I generate more reviews on For Free with Seller Central?

When you are logged into Seller Central, first go to the menu for "Orders" → "Manage Orders" and then select either "View FBA Orders" or "View Seller Fulfilled Orders." From here, a drop down of orders with a default to the last 7 days of sales will appear. You will see the order details including the order number and "Buyer Name." Select the buyer's name highlighted in blue. A new box will open.

Under "Subject," there will be a drop-down menu, change this to "Feedback Request." From here you can use a standard script which you will write and save either in your saved templates in SC or somewhere on the computer of whoever manages your customer service. It is a time-consuming job, but you can initially contact each customer this way. Be assumptive and ask how they are enjoying their product, ask if you can answer any product questions, remind them of the product warranty and your great customer service, and how to reach customer service should any future questions arise. Then provide a link back to the product page from which they purchased and ask if they would please leave positive feedback for the product so that other customers can find it more easily. Thank them profusely for their help. Make it as easy as possible and do as much of the work for them. You can also let them know that they can go back to their recent orders online or in the app to click on the product and leave a review that way. This way you have provided several easy options for them to hopefully leave you a positive review and/or give you the opportunity to "make it right" before they leave a dissatisfactory review.

How Can I Generate More Reviews with An Outside Service?

There are a number of services out there that provide template-based solutions to managing all of your feedback requests. If you Google "generate Amazon feedback" or "get Amazon reviews" or something of the like, you will populate a number of services that can manage reviews for you.

One of the ones I really like is JungleScout Launch, Helium 10 has a great one, Feedback Genius by Seller Labs is another one, Sales Backer has a good tool that is easy to use. I would look at all of your options and compare pricing before you decide.

HACK # 21 - Go with email automation as opposed to the free models because it will run on autopilot and increase your reviews significantly without maintenance!

The extra bonus for many of these service providers is they will give you access to other great free tools such as keyword planning, automatic listing optimizations, analytics, and product research.

You will have really unique data and insights that many of your competitors won't have! Sometimes you can even get crucial sales estimator data from your competitors unbeknownst to them. Obviously, this data is all public, nothing private is shared, but the for the average person they would not know how to discover this data on their own.

Store Feedback is often missed, I find that most of my clients don't even know it exists. If you go under the "Performance" → "Feedback" menu you will find it. Navigate to this sub-menu and you will be at your Feedback Manager panel.

From here you will be able to see your outstanding Feedback Rating, how many ratings you have, including positive, neutral, and negative. In the middle left of the page you will see "Recent Feedback" and this becomes rather important. The report can be downloaded for review with team members, but I do want to draw your attention to the right side of the page where it shows "Actions" and to "Chose One" with a drop-down menu.

It is important to be reviewing this feedback regularly. For many of the good ones, you can either express your thanks or leave them unattended. Note that whatever you post will be public and that if someone on Amazon were to click on your store front and read those reviews, they will also see your replies. The same goes for managing the neutral and the negative feedback.

Let us first discuss the negative feedback, as these are the most damaging. The light at the end of the tunnel is many of these will either be automatically mitigated by Amazon. Their algorithm will pre-screen the customer responses and if they see that the poor review is in regard to FBA fulfillment performance for example, the negative review will automatically be removed.

Many customers accidentally leave a product review here, in your store feedback, rather than on the product detail page. This is because some customers are confused between feedback and product reviews. In the event you see negative product reviews in your store feedback you can select the right hand "Chose One" → "Request Removal." A message will appear that says:

"Amazon only removes feedback in the following cases:

- The feedback includes obscene language.

- The feedback includes seller-specific personally identifiable information.

- The entire feedback comment is a product review.

- Strike through feedback if it is regarding fulfillment or customer service for an order fulfilled by Amazon.

Did the feedback you received meet any of the criteria above?"

HACK # 22 - You are going to Select "Yes"

If the removal of this review is successful, you will see a message display that says the following:

"We have reviewed this feedback and found it does not comply with our policies, so we have struck-it through. View case"

If you see this message, Congratulations! You have successfully removed a negative rating from your store, thereby increASINg your star-average.

In the event the message is not removed, you will see the below message:

"We have reviewed this feedback and found that it is not in violation of our guidelines and has been retained. To request further review of this decision, re-open the case in Case Log. View case"

If this happens do not be discouraged, it means you have the opportunity to post a public reply to the customer and try to offer a solution where both parties feel better. You can write something along the lines of what we discussed earlier in this chapter about "make-goods" when posting public replies to customer reviews when they are unhappy. Always apologize, be charming, offer a solution, and multiple ways for the customer to contact you via email and or phone.

You can do this by Selecting "Chose One" → "Post a public reply"

Dealing with neutral reviews will be the same process. I recommend you first attempt to remove all negative and neutral reviews, and if they cannot be removed then you will want to reply to all neutral or negative reviews.

Your Feedback Manager will not be very busy, you will accrue far fewer store feedback ratings than product reviews so this feature will be less to manage. I encourage you to check it daily though this way you do not leave any unhappy customers unattended for weeks.

REPORTING BASICS

I will go into my favorite and what I find the most useful data within this section so that you are not overwhelmed with numbers. Sometimes you need to weed through all of the information and acronyms to get to the most important info. Personally, I think there are four areas of importance; the rest is cake toppers (CTR, Average Sale per Order, Average units per order, Impressions). So many of these other metrics are nice to have but do not always help you sell more or plan for growth. That is why I look at them as sprinkles on the cake. If you are looking for the cake, I go with these suggestions.

Within the "Reports" → "Business Reports" tab you will have access to the most important metrics. You can also access this same page from your home screen where it says "Sales Summary" and then you can click the link for "View more of your sales statistics." Both ways navigate to the same reporting.

These are the basic reports which you have access to as a professional seller. The Sales and Traffic Report will give you sales data by date, which can be modified. It can go as short as a one-day period or as long as a two-year snapshot. Reports can be modified and downloaded using the controls in the upper right-hand corner above the graph.

HACK # 23 - I find that a lot of my customers like to the default "Sales Dashboard" view and change the dates to look at daily sales, or sales last week or month.

The Detail Page Sales and Traffic by Child Item report will give you sales broken down by ASIN. This way you can see specifically what your best-selling items are and record their sales by week, month, or year. Be sure to download these reports regularly so that you can keep good historical sales records for each ASIN and/or parent (depending on how you would prefer to track).

You can monitor your seller performance (based on sales), view excess inventory and recommended actions, view notifications on any recommended operational improvements (such as fixing stranded inventory) and Restock Inventory.

HACK # 24 - The Restock Inventory is really the most relevant for our purposes of planning and forecasting. This nifty tool will tell you exactly how many units it's expecting to sell over the next 30 days. It takes into consideration your lead times, tells you exactly when to ship the product to the FBA warehouse and how many units of each ASIN to ship. This information is currently available under the menu for "Inventory" → "Inventory Planning" → "Restock Inventory."

Always remember the recommendations can potentially be misleading, and it is self-learning. This tool assumes a constant demand. If you are expecting a slow down or an increase in demand that the system would not know about (promotions, advertising, unforeseen price changes up or down), then it would not be able to account for that. Don't rely 100% on this data, use your best judgment. If you are going through a big growth cycle and you have good performance index scoring (excess of 350 points), then you can and should listen to the forecast prediction. If you are anticipating any kind of slow down due to price increases, or shifts in demand caused by external factors, then you need to put your conservative hat on.

The Inventory Performance Index (IPI) matters, you have to keep within good standing performance otherwise you could potentially face short-term and long-term excessive inventory warehousing fees. The higher your score, the less likely that you will incur any type of charges, but if you send too much inventory to Amazon and it is not selling, I would expect your score to gradually decline under 350 points and make you susceptible to fees for warehousing outside of traditional fulfillment fees.

Just remember it is better to be conservative than overzealous. You can always prepare another FBA shipment quickly and have it in the FC within two weeks. As long as you are monitoring your fulfillment data/performance, then you should not have any issues.

If ever you need to increase your seller performance in a pinch, you can perform one of three functions:

- Create a removal order to get yourself to a more conservative position in FBA.

SELLING ON AMAZON: 2020 HACKS

- Create a sale on the product to encourage more orders.
- Create an ad on the products to get more glance views (impressions) which = sales.

It is important to understand these influences on the Amazon Forecasting Tools:

1. In-Stock Rate

2. Price Consistency (Up, down, same)

3. Historical Demand

4. Promotions

5. Seasonality

6. Traffic (Organic, internal or external advertising)

Keep in mind that all forecasting data provided by Amazon is updated daily so make sure that it is being checked and/or analyzed regularly. Do not put this function on auto-pilot because the numbers can and do change, especially if you are growing. Remember that it is possible to beat your forecast. Alternatively, out of stock periods are bad and can slow an ASIN's rank even for a short period of time. Always keep the pipeline full. Avoid outages that can hurt your ASIN's sales momentum and relevance.

PAYMENTS

The payments menu is fairly easy to use as well. It can be located by "Reports" → "Payments" or from the home page when you login to Seller Central on the right-hand side under "Payments Summary" → "View Payments Summary." Both options take you to the same place. As you have no doubt discovered Amazon will pay you in two-week cycles.

The default payments menu will be on "Statement View" but you can also change the view if you wanted to see each transaction, or a history of statements, or just your advertising spends. From this primary payment menu, you can literally see every dollar in and out for your Seller Central store.

On the statement view, the top of the menu will tell you what you are outstanding and the next transfer date and the rest of the screen will be a basic accounting ledger of your credits and debts to the account including Amazon fees, rebates, promos, product charges, advertising (if billed against remittance), FBA fees, and lastly what you can expect to be paid.

If you would like to update any of your banking or credit card information please make sure to navigate to the upper right side of the screen and then "Settings" → "Account Info" → "Payment Information."

Payment Information Includes:

- Deposit Methods

- Charge Methods

- Invoiced Order Payments Method

- Charge Methods for Advertising

HACK # 25 - Did you know you can pay for all of your advertising against remittance? Click on "Charge Methods for Advertising" to change your payment setting to "Seller Account Method" if you do not want to pay for ads via credit card.

While you are in the Seller Account Information menu it is a good time to review all of this information to make sure that your store is not missing any crucial info. Some of these important sub-menus include:

- Business Address

- Return Address

- Shipping Settings

- Your Seller Profile (which is your store name customers will see on the detail page)

RETURNS

The returns process is fairly simple in Seller Central. Let's first make sure you have your return address correctly setup in the system. Navigate to "Settings" → "Account Info" → "Shipping and Return Information" → "Return Address." This should take you to a "General Settings" screen where you can choose to receive return request emails, automatically authorize returns, and whether or not you want to provide an RMA number (return merchandise authorization) to Amazon or let them generate one.

You can also include a little blurb about your return policies and Amazon shoppers will see this under your store info publicly on the site. If you include nothing in this field the default Amazon Policies will apply. I would suggest you do not tell customers that they will have a re-stocking fee because they generally will be upset when they find this out after the fact.

There is a sub-menu for return-less refunds, which means the customer gets a partial refund and can keep or discard the product. In the event a customer is not happy or the item is broken, you will just refund them automatically a percentage of the product value rather than get the item back to your warehouse. This also prevents additional return fees affiliated with returning the product to the FBA warehouse.

The last sub-menu is your "Return Address Settings" and this is an important one that is frequently missed during setup. You will need to provide Amazon with an address if you are to expect any returns, so make sure your default address is correct and up to date. If you have more than one address you can also enter that here, look to the right where it says, "Do you have more than one return address?"

HACK # 26 - You can set yourself up to receive automatic un-fulfillable returns via FBA every week so that you do not need to manually do this every week!

Navigate to "Settings" → "Fulfillment by Amazon" and you will see all of your defaulted FBA settings.

Now go mid-way down and look for "Automated Unfulfillable Removal Settings" make sure you have this enabled. This will guarantee that all unfulfillable inventory is automatically removed and returned to you each week.

You can also put the long-term storage removals on auto-pilot as well by enabling the next topic down which is "Automated Long-Term Storage Removals Settings." This will remove units subject to long-term storage fees.

(Your FBA barcode labeling settings are also included in this menu if you ever need to find them, under FBA Product Barcode Preference.)

THE 1 HOUR PLAN

By now you are wondering, how does this tie together, and what is the 1-hour plan? The ground work was laid out in previous chapters so you understand where everything is and how it all functions. You have to develop a good sense of direction in order to get efficient and fast at managing your business in Seller Central, and it is also true that there is a lot of fluff in there. It seems overwhelming because in their attempt to make it easy, they provided 2-4 ways to reach the same information, thereby creating confusion. Your fall back should always be the Help section or "Get Support."

HACK # 27 - If you are ever lost it is ok to stop and ask for directions, that is basically what the ticket system was designed for.

Below is your check list in order of importance when you login every day:

1. Buyer Seller Messages - Message on Home Screen of Amazon. Reply to each in the Target 24 hr period to keep a good rating with customers. Even my highest volume brands never have more than a few messages a day, outside of holiday season. Can also reach this screen from the

"Messages" link on the upper right corner of every page. **TOTAL TIME = 2-5 minutes**

2. View your Store Feedback - check and reply to any new neutral or negative feedback. Request removal for any that don't belong. ("Performance" → "Feedback") **TOTAL TIME = 2-5 minutes**

3. Respond to Product Reviews – Check for and reply to any poor product reviews ("Performance" → "Voice of the Customer", and "Performance" → "Brand Dashboard" → Critical Customer Reviews). **TOTAL TIME** = 0-7 minutes depending on if there are any

4. Sales Report for Last day, week, month - View Sales Summary on home screen in Seller Central. If you want to see activity by day or per ASIN then click "View more of your statistics" and from here toggle to the sales dashboard and change the dates to yesterday. Once a month download the entire product sales by child ASIN report for the entire previous month and file this. **TOTAL TIME = 5-7 Minutes**

5. Check your forecast - You will want to look at your product restock report ("Inventory" → "Inventory Planning"). If you are running low send more inventory in. I like to look at the report once a week on Monday AM. **TOTAL TIME = 1-2 Minutes**

6. Advertising - Optimize ads once every 7-14 days. If any of the ads have high ACOS they may need more attention, if you have more than 6 campaigns It could also take more time. **TOTAL TIME** = 10-30 minutes once a week! This equates to under 5 minutes per day on average.

HACK # 28 - You can look for services that do automatic ad optimizations for you, this means you will never have to optimize your own ads every again (only approve optimizations)! They are paid services; you can Google automatic PPC optimizations. OptMyAds is one of them. **TOTAL TIME** = 5-15 minutes one or twice a week! This takes 0-1 minute per day on average!

7. Adjust Inventory - If you are using FBM you will want to peek at inventory once per day to make sure there are no mistakes. **TOTAL TIME = 1-5 minutes.**

8. Send Inventory to FBA - This assumes you have already converted your ASIN to FBA. Create shipment once per month at most to send inventory to FBA. ("Inventory" → "Manage FBA Shipments" → "Send to Amazon") **TOTAL TIME = 30 minutes per month MAX. This is only 1 minute per day averaged across an entire month!**

9. Review Request Emails - If you have selected the automated route, then you have chosen to set it and forget it. Never make another manual request again! **TOTAL TIME = 0 Minutes per day!**

10. Manage Returns - If you have enabled automatic RMA and automatic removal of unfulfillable inventory then you never have to make another return request by hand again. **TOTAL TIME = 0 minutes per day!**

11. Schedule deals (optional) - Try to slot your deals in quarters, so you will work on this once per quarter. It will cut down on the labor by a lot and give you a complete plan

that executes itself. ("Advertising" → "Deals" or "Advertising" → "Promotions"). **TOTAL TIME = 15-30 minutes once every three months.**

12. IPI Health - The goal is to stay in the green. Your Inventory Performance Index is based on how well you keep popular products in stock, maintain healthy inventory levels, and fix listing problems. If you spot issues, deal with them early. The IPI threshold for store limits is a score of 400, you want to ideally be over 700. If it's less, make some adjustments. The system will advise what adjustments to make on each ASIN's. ("Inventory" → "Inventory Planning" → "Inventory Performance Index"). **TOTAL TIME = 1-5 minutes per week.**

13. Payments - Keeping track of what you are spending and what Amazon owes you is always good to know. They pay every two weeks, so every couple of weeks spend a few minutes reviewing and then check for any discrepancies. ("Reports" → "Payments"). **TOTAL TIME = 5 minutes once every other week.**

14. Manage Brand - If you have completed your brand page and checked your ASIN byline links, you can just keep watching it once a week or so. This takes no time practically. Check your Account Health screen periodically for alerts ("Performance" → "Account Health").

15. Pricing Health - "Automate Pricing" matches the lowest buy box offer and creates rules so that you can increase your buy box percentage in the event there are several resellers with fluctuating prices. You don't need to automate

the entire catalog. ("Pricing" → "Automate Pricing"). **TOTAL TIME** = 0-2 minutes per week!

16. CASES - these will be as needed, but if you are like me you are creating 1-2 a week for troubleshooting. Go with the email version unless it's an emergency. ("Help" → "Get Support"). **TOTAL TIME** = 2-5 minutes once per week.

Once you get good at going through this list you will be able to manage your account in well under 1 hour per day. You will hammer out each piece, working down the list. Eventually you will be a lot more confident in where you need to go to manage each part of Seller Central. The bare minimum would take about 30 minutes per day on average.

HACK # 29 - Use the Seller University! Go to "Performance" → "Seller University" to learn more and watch videos on literally every topic relating to your Seller Central Account.

HACK #30 - Did you know you can request that Amazon review your FBA fees, and then be reimbursed on overcharges? Make a ticket under "Fulfillment by Amazon" → "Investigate Other FBA Issues" → "Confirm/Request Reimbursement for Product Weights and Dimensions" and ask them to remeasure your ASINS to reduce your fees! You may unlock hidden money.

TIPS & TRICKS

1) Free Keyword Tools: help find keywords to implement on front and back end

- Google Keyword Planner Tool
- https://keywordtool.io/Amazon
- https://www.merchantwords.com/
- https://moz.com/free-seo-tools
- When on Amazon, search #keyword to come up with a list of other most popular keywords. For example, search #robots, then write down all of the other terms and use on your hidden keywords or in content.
- KW Index Checker - it's an APP for Chrome. (fee may be applicable)

2) Discover what product categories or products are hot:

- https://www.junglescout.com/
- https://amzscout.net/

3) Track Pricing and Rank History of any ASIN on Amazon.com

- www.camelcamelcamel.com
- www.keepa.com

4) Fake Review Analyzer

- https://www.fakespot.com/
- https://reviewmeta.com/

5) Generate More Reviews on Seller Central

- www.helium10.com
- www.junglescout.com
- www.salesbacker.com
- www.sellerlabs.com

6) Help for Removing Sellers and Navigating Brand Issues on Amazon.com

- https://potoosolutions.com/

7) Seller Forums

- https://sellercentral.Amazon.com/forums/

8) Amazon Advertising YouTube Channel:

- Visit YouTube and search "Amazon Advertising Channel."

9) LinkedIn Groups:

- Amazon Vendor Central (AVC)
- Amazon Seller Central (ASC)
- Search more Amazon groups for Valuable Q&A
- Add me on LinkedIn https://www.linkedin.com/in/awilkens/10)

10) PPC Automations:

- www.optmyads.com

- www.teikametrics.com

- www.sellics.com

11) Please see my other book available in print and kindle on Amazon:

- "Become a Bestseller on Amazon.com"

Contact me for Consulting or Rep Services:

- www.dotcomreps.com

- Email: adam@dotcomreps.com

I would love to hear from you!

GLOSSARY

1P - 1st Party, referring to Vendor Central. Also referred to as a "Retail" vendor.

3P - 3rd Party, referring to Seller Central. Also referred to as a "Marketplace" supplier.

A+ - Also called Enhanced Brand Content. Offers a digital brochure for your product(s) on the detail page below the standard product description.

a9 - the SEO language specific to the Amazon.com platform. See www.a9.com

ACOS - Advertising Cost of Sale.

ACPC - Average Cost per Click.

Amazoninians - Describes people who work for Amazon.com. The Amazon company culture.

AMG - Amazon Media Group, the display advertising team.

AMS - Amazon Marketing Services, now called Amazon Advertising.

ARA - Amazon Retail Analytics.

ASIN - Amazon Standard Identification Number. The Amazon Standard Identification Number is a 10-character alphanumeric unique identifier assigned by Amazon.com and its partners for product identification within the Amazon organization

ASN - Advance Shipment Notification.

ASP - Average Selling Price.

B2C - Business to Consumer.

BD - Best Deal.

BIN Check - If ever you need to request an Amazon review, the correct product is in the network at the FC you would request a Bin Check. This is when their warehouse associates confirm the product in the Bin is the correct product the customer receives when they place an order for a given ASIN. It is a quality control check at the FC of inventory correctness.

BOL - Bill of Lading.

Brand Registry - Service that offers additional brand tools and protection for manufacturers with intellectual property.

Browse Nodes - The specific selling category assigned to your product. i.e., "Sporting Goods" → "Bicycles" → "Mountain Bicycles".

Buy Box - The owner of the primary sales offer on the Detail Page.

CARP - Carrier Appointment Request Portal. Does not apply to the marketplace.

CM - Category Manager, aka Vendor Manager.

COGS - Cost of Goods Sold.

COOP - Cooperative Marketing Allowance or Funding for Deals, Promotions, or Discounts.

CPC - Cost Per Click.

CPM - Technically this means "Cost per Mile," but it is most frequently used to refer to Cost Per Thousand, as it concerns advertising impressions. i.e., Cost per thousand impressions.

CRAP - Can't Realize Any Profit. A Term used when your ASIN economics have been deemed unprofitable by Amazon.

CSLD - Category Specific Lighting Deal.

CTA - Call to Action. Marketing Terminology to prompt customers to "act" on a deal or special price.

CTR - Click through Rate. % of people who an ad made an impression on and clicked on ad.

DA - Damage Allowance. This is an allowance in Vendor Central. Does not apply to the marketplace.

Detail Page - The independent page that houses all of your ASIN content, outfacing to the customer.

DMM - Divisional Merchandising Manager. Above the VM and the VMM.

DOTD - Deal of the Day.

Duplicate - A double or copy of the same product with a different ASIN on Amazon.com

EBC - Enhanced Brand Content, also called A+ content. Offers a digital brochure for your product(s) on the detail page below the standard product description.

FA - Freight Allowance.

FBA - Fulfilled by Amazon (Seller Central). Amazon ships the order to the customer.

FBM - Fulfilled by Merchant (Seller Central, B2C). Seller Drop-ships to the customer.

FC - Fulfilment Center.

Gateway Page - Referring to the home page that you land on for www.Amazon.com

Gating - Blocking specific sellers from reselling your products or brands. Part of Brand Registry.

GBLD - Gold Box Lighting Deal.

GL - The primary selling category where your products can be found on Amazon.com.

Halo Effect - The Residual Euphoric Sales Lift an ASIN has after a faster turn rate caused by lower price or increased traffic to the detail page.

Hero ASIN - In a promotion, this refers to the ASIN primary out facing product exposed to the customer of a grouping. It is usually your best seller in a group.

HSA - Headline Search Ads. These ads appear under the search bar. Now called a sponsored brand ad.

Hybrid - A manufacturer who simultaneously operates Vendor Central and Seller Central accounts.

IPI - Inventory Performance Index.

ISM - In-Stock Manager. This position within merchandising helps with ops related issues such as purchase order troubleshooting and forecasting.

LBB - Lost Buy Box. Amazon refers to this figure as a % of time that you do not own the Buy Box.

MAP - Minimum Advertised Pricing.

MDF - Market Development Funding (Coop). This is an allowance in Vendor Central. Does not apply to marketplace.

Merge - Combining two ASINs into one. Or movement of any information from one place to another.

MSRP - Manufacturer Suggested Retail Price.

NIS - New Item Setup. Refers to the XML setup files by category in Seller Central by which you can create new ASIN's

OOS - Out of Stock.

OPS - Amazon uses this term internally regarding "Sales."

PCOGS - Net Sales. This stands for product cost of goods sold.

PDA - Product Display Ads. These ads appear on detail pages under buying options.

Platform - Also see UI. It is the name given to the Amazon.com site and sister sites.

POC - Point of Contact, refers to your main contact in an organization.

POD - Proof of Delivery (request).

RA - Return Allowance. This is an allowance in Vendor Central. Does not apply to marketplace.

RANK - Refers to your sales rank number in a category relative to all others in that category.

RMA - Return Merchandise Authorization.

ROAS - Return on Ad Spend (similar to ROI).

RR - Routing Request. Relating to shipment requests in Vendor Central. Does not apply to marketplace.

SBV - Sponsored Brand Video Ad, formally VIS.

SC - Seller Central.

SDP - Shortage Dispute Process. Another form of POD in Vendor Central. Does not apply to marketplace, but there are shortages and a process for disputing receiving issues in the marketplace.

SERP - Search Engine Page Results.

Shoveler - Widgets on Amazon.com facing the customer that provide purchASINg suggestions based on customer metrics, current promos, or best performers in a group.

SOP - Standard Operating Procedures.

SPA - Sponsored Product Ads. These Ads appear in Search Results.

SP - Selling Price.

SKU - Stock Keeping unit. Your manufacturer assigned a model number.

Store Page - AKA brand page. This is the storefront page you create for your brand (must be resisted).

Twister - Also known as a "Variation." This is a grouping of like ASIN's that are combined into one detail page and are differentiated by size, color, or style.

UI - user Interface. The term Amazon uses to describe any of their various websites.

Vine - Paid program for generating approved reviews through Vendor Central. The marketplace equivalent is ERP (earlier reviewer program).

VIS - Video in Search. Amazon's latest AMS tool which adds a short video as a sponsored product ad. Now referred to as a sponsored brand video

VLT - Vendor Lead Times.

VM - Vendor Manager, synonymous with Category Manager.

VMM - Vendor Manager, Manager. A manager of Vendor Managers.

VPC - Vendor Powered Coupons

VC - Vendor Central. This is the retail side of Amazon when they own your goods. Also called 1P.

VSS - Vendor Self Service, references the Vendor Central uI platform. Does not apply to the marketplace.

WOC - Weeks of Cover. Refers to how many weeks of inventory usage based on sales.

WOW - Week on Week. Referencing sales comparing the current week to week prior.

YOY - Year on Year. Comparing sales from one year to the next.

NOTES

NOTES

_____

_____

_____

_____

_____

_____

_____

_____

_____

_____

_____

_____

Made in the USA
Monee, IL
25 July 2020